2

Sandra Salmandjee
Photos: Patrice Hauser
Food styling: Sophie Dupuis-Gaulier

INDIA!

Recipes from the
Bollywood Kitchen

h.f.ullmann

Contents

Swaajat!*

Sandra Salmandjee
a.k.a. Sanjee

Her modern and inventive style of Indian cuisine takes us on an exotic voyage of discovery. Sandra Salmandjee (also known as Chef Sanjee) appeals to a range of discerning tastes, with recipes based on the specialties of a country that reflects her own personality—a kaleidoscope of smiles, pleasure, colors, sharing, and gastronomy. She obviously knows all there is to know about coriander, ginger, and turmeric, as the way she uses these and other spices is exceptional. Cooking is passed on in her family through diverse cultures, and is enriched by them: a pinch of French cuisine (she lives in France) combined, most importantly, with a generous bowl of Indian flavors that have been passed down from her ancestors.

Indian cuisine

Comparing an Indian meal with a Western one is no easy task, as the concept of starter—main dish—dessert does not really exist in India. The meal usually begins with a little tidbit, often sweet, to whet the appetite. Flavors are combined by serving all the dishes together on the table or on a *thali* (a large platter with compartments). The flavors balance naturally during the course of the meal: sweet, bitter, salty, pungent, sour, and astringent. These six aspects of taste form the basis of Ayurveda (the science of longevity) and are the daily prerequisite for maintaining good health. It is all eaten together in small mouthfuls, scooped up with the fingers and a chapati (flatbread). Indian cuisine is elegant but very simple, once you have mastered the basics. Join me on this gourmet journey to discover the best Indian recipes.

Rolling pin and board
(chakla) for chapatis

Frying
pan

Tawa (flat pan for
making flatbreads)

Small frying pan for tarka
(i.e. tempering spices)

Skimmer for fritters
and wooden tongs

Pestle and mortar
for spices

Chopping board

Ladle

Rice spoon

Knife

Utensils

Pan

Ingredients

You will need a few essential items to get you started with Indian cooking: tamarind paste, chickpea (gram) flour, curry leaves, and of course Basmati rice ... These are becoming easier to find in specialized Indian or Asian stores, and even on the internet. My favorite websites are set out at the end of the book.

Ginger

Garlic

Eggplants

Red onions

Chilis

Small green mangoes

Concentrated tomato paste

Atta (chapati flour)

Chickpea (gram) flour

Limes

Green onions

Shallots

Almonds

Asafetida
(powdered gum resin)

Kaffir lime

Curry leaves

Spring roll pastry

Ghee
(clarified butter)

Okra (lady's fingers)

Sweetened condensed milk

Coconut milk

Cashew nuts

Paneer

Papadum

Basmati rice

Cornstarch

White sesame seeds

Garlic paste

Mango pulp

Lentils

Mango chutney

Pistachios

Coconut milk powder

Rose syrup

Tamarind paste

Black tea

Star anise

Cinnamon

Cardamom

Turmeric

Turmeric powder

Fenugreek

Bay leaf

Nutmeg

Paprika

Cloves

White pepper

Cumin

Garam masala

Yellow mustard seeds

Black mustard seeds

Chili powder

Ground ginger

Saffron

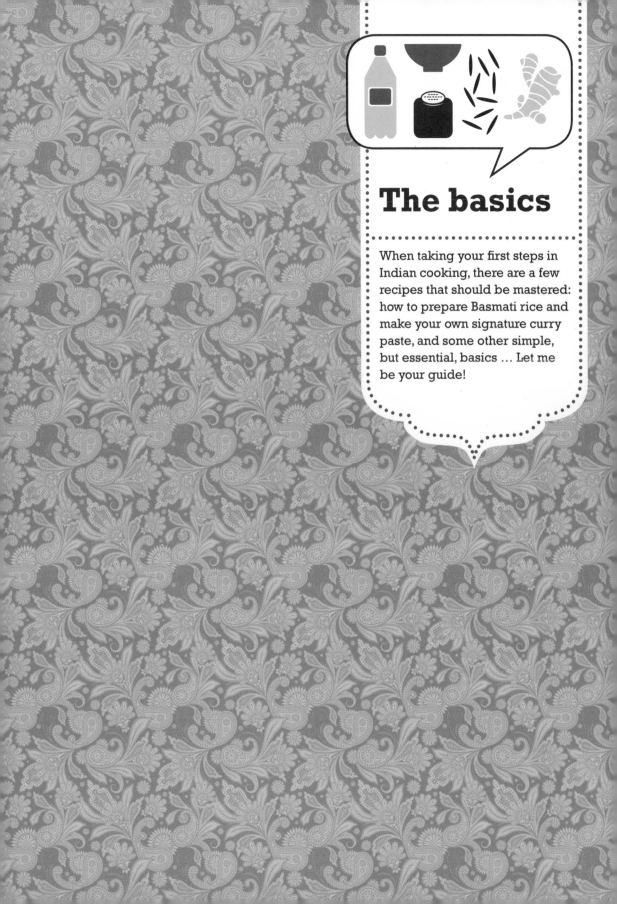

The basics

When taking your first steps in Indian cooking, there are a few recipes that should be mastered: how to prepare Basmati rice and make your own signature curry paste, and some other simple, but essential, basics ... Let me be your guide!

Basmati rice

All the recipes in this book use the famous Basmati rice, the only one I ever reach for when cooking.

Rice plays an important role in the Indian diet, especially in the south of the country, where it is grown. It is not always eaten every single day as it is a fairly expensive item, so it is a special feature on the dinner table, equal in importance to any other dish.

Indians eat rice with dahl (lentils), providing large amounts of the amino acids (complete proteins) that are essential for a healthy diet.

Basmati is premium grade rice, so it tends to be used on special occasions (parties, birthdays, weddings, etc.) in the form of biryanis (see p. 100).

Basmati rice keeps very well, and even improves with age! It is available from Indian grocery stores, delicatessens, and supermarkets.

Rice is also used to make flour, and even batter for pancakes and fritters.

Indians eat Basmati almost exclusively; it is one of the 42,000 varieties of rice found across the globe.

How to cook rice

Preparation: 10 minutes
Cooking time: 15–20 minutes
Resting time: 10 minutes

1¼ cups (250 g) Basmati rice
generous 1½ cups (375 ml)
 water
scant ½ tsp fine salt

Ingredients to serve 4

Rinse the rice several times in cold water, draining it each time, until the water runs clear. It will be clean and white and the grains will not stick together. If you have time, leave it to soak for a few hours, then the grains will visibly lengthen by 20–25 percent, depending on the quality of the rice.

To use the steam method, put the stated amounts of rice and water into a pan. Add salt, cover with a lid, and simmer for 15–20 minutes (the length of time will vary according to the quantity of rice and thickness of the pan).

The steam cooks the rice as the water is being absorbed by the grains. Never take the lid off the pan before the end of the cooking time as the steam will escape and the cooking process will be affected.

When the rice is cooked, turn off the heat and leave it for about 10 minutes, still covered.

Carefully fluff up the rice with a fork, making sure you do not break the grains.

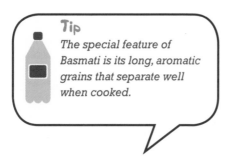

Tip

The special feature of Basmati is its long, aromatic grains that separate well when cooked.

Preparation: 5 minutes
Cooking time: 18 minutes
Resting time: 10 minutes

5 cardamom pods
1⅓ cups (250 g) cooked
   Basmati rice
scant ½ tsp fine salt

Ingredients to serve 4

Cardamom rice
Cardamom pulao

Place the cardamom pods in a piece of muslin and tie it up with string.

Cook the rice in a pan with generous 1½ cups (375 ml) water, cardamom pods, and salt. Cover and cook on medium heat for about 18 minutes.

When cooked, turn off the heat and allow the rice to rest, covered, for another 10 minutes.

Tip
The muslin makes it easy to remove the pods after cooking, but it is not essential.

Spices

As well as having health-giving properties (good for the digestion, as well as being antioxidants and even healing agents), spices imbue dishes with wonderful aromas, colors, and flavors.

The essential Indian spices are turmeric, coriander, cumin, fenugreek, cardamom, cloves, cinnamon, dried chili, and pepper. Completing the list are other spices that are just as interesting, if less common: mustard seeds, fennel, nutmeg, and saffron, amongst others.

From two to five different spices—if not more—are often used in one dish.

Then there are the spice blends usually made by the women of the household, including the famous garam masala. Literally meaning "hot" (*garam*) and "mixture" (*masala*), the version used here is made up of black pepper, cumin, cloves, cardamom, cinnamon, and bay leaves. The spices are used either whole or ground, and in varying proportions. This makes each garam masala unique to the individual cook.

Here is my own recipe for garam masala: 2 teaspoons of black pepper, 3 teaspoons of cumin seeds, 1 teaspoon of cloves, 1 teaspoon of cardamom seeds, 1 cinnamon stick, and 2–3 bay leaves. You can grind these spices or leave them whole.

The commercial curry powder found in stores is also a mixture of these essential spices.

Curry paste

This paste forms the basis of many Indian dishes. You can use it to make chicken tikka (see recipe on p. 88).

You can also make a very quick meal by mixing it with generous ¾ cup (200 ml) of coconut milk and browning 1 cup (200 g) of shredded chicken breast in this mixture.

Firstly, make a cashew nut cream. Soak cashew nuts in 1 generous cup (250 ml) of water for 1 hour, then whizz them well in a food mixer or chopper until you have a smooth, thick cream.

Fry the whole spices in a large pan for 5 minutes on high heat in 4 tablespoons of vegetable oil.

Add the chopped onions and green chili (de-seeded and finely chopped) and cook for 10 minutes, stirring all the time, until the onions are translucent.

Add the puréed garlic and ginger, along with all the ground spices and 1 teaspoon of fine salt. Mix well and thin with ⅔ cup (150 ml) of water. When the liquid has evaporated, add the tomato paste and cashew cream. Reduce again for 10 minutes on medium heat.

Preparation + cooking time: 35 minutes
Resting time: 1 hour

Ingredients for 1 x 9 oz (250 g) jar

3 tbsp (20 g) cashew nuts (untoasted and unsalted)
whole spices: 3 cardamom pods, 2 cloves, 2 bay leaves
4 yellow onions, chopped
1 green chili (optional)
4 garlic cloves or 1 tbsp garlic paste (see recipe on p. 26)
1½ inch (4 cm) piece ginger root or 1 tbsp ginger paste
ground spices: 1 tsp garam masala, 1 tbsp cumin, 1 tbsp coriander, ½ tsp turmeric
3 tbsp concentrated tomato paste
vegetable oil
salt

Tip
The curry paste will keep in the fridge for a week to 10 days, and can also be frozen.

Ingredients for 1 x 9 oz (250 g) jar of paste

Garlic paste
9 oz (250 g) garlic
4–5 tbsp vegetable oil

Ginger paste
9 oz (250 g) organic fresh
   ginger root
4–5 tbsp vegetable oil

Garlic and ginger pastes

Garlic and ginger form the basis of most Indian dishes. Using them every day is generally easier when they are available in paste form. You can make a mixed paste of equal parts garlic and ginger. In curry recipes this paste can replace fresh garlic (1 teaspoon of garlic paste is equivalent to 3 garlic cloves) and fresh ginger (1 teaspoon of ginger paste is equivalent to a 1 in / 3 cm piece of ginger root).

Garlic paste: peel the garlic cloves and remove any green central shoots. Whizz in a food mixer with some vegetable oil.

Ginger paste: peel the ginger root. Whizz in a food mixer with some vegetable oil.

Tip
These pastes will keep in the refrigerator for 3–4 weeks in a glass jar with a lid. Cover the paste with a drizzle of vegetable oil to prevent it from spoiling in contact with the air.

Paneer

Paneer is the only cheese found in India, and is made with whole cow's milk. It is eaten either in solid form or cubed, and often fried in ghee; or melted and used to bind the sauce in specific dishes.

Bring the milk to the boil, watching it carefully. Turn off the heat as soon as it boils and add the vinegar. Allow the milk to curdle for 10 minutes.

Strain the cheese through a piece of muslin. Retain the liquid, squeezing the muslin to get as much out of the cheese as possible.

Leave the paneer in the cloth, shaping it like a chunky flattened pebble, or put it in any container you like. If you stop at this stage, you will have fresh paneer to bind your sauces.

Place a weight on top of the container. Leave the paneer to rest in the cloth under the weight for 30 minutes. Remove the paneer from the cloth, cover it in plastic wrap, and refrigerate for 30 minutes.

Your paneer is now ready. Chop it into approximately ¾ in (2 cm) square cubes.

Do not try to replace the whole milk with low-fat milk as you may obtain only a very small amount of paneer.

Preparation: 10 minutes
Cooking time: 5 minutes
Resting time: 1 hour

1 quart (1 liter) whole milk
3 tbsp white wine vinegar
1 piece of muslin (or a kitchen cloth)

Ingredients for approx. 5 oz (150 g) fresh paneer

Tip
Paneer will keep for 1 week in the refrigerator in the retained liquid, or simply in some cold water. It can also be frozen.

Ghee
Clarified butter

In India, ghee (clarified butter) is used on a daily basis for all types of cooking, in either savory or sweet recipes. This cooked butter, with its proteins removed, unlike ordinary butter makes it possible to fry spices without burning them.

Cook the coarsely chopped butter in a thick-bottomed pan for 45–60 minutes (depending on the water content of the butter you use) on medium heat. Skim off any sediment as it develops on the butter.

When the butter is cooked, strain it to get rid of the sediment, using a piece of butter muslin or a very fine-mesh strainer.

Pour the ghee into a glass jar with a lid. Once it has cooled down, store it in the fridge (where it will set) or at room temperature.

In India, ghee is regarded as more than just a fat. It is above all refreshing—unlike oil, which increases heat. And as it cooks, ghee absorbs and enhances the beneficial properties of food and spices—unlike oil, which changes them.

Tip
You can buy ready-prepared ghee in stores and keep it at room temperature.

Preparation: 10 minutes
Cooking time: 45 minutes to 1 hour

2¼ cups (500 g) organic butter
1 butter muslin or very fine-mesh strainer to filter the butter

Ingredients for 2¼ cups (500 g) ghee

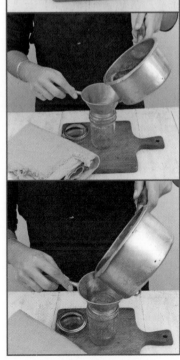

Tamarind
chutney

Coconut
chutney

Mint
chutney

Cilantro
chutney

Chutneys

Mango
chutney

Useful fact

*Chutney is used as a
condiment with practically
every Indian meal. It adds
balance, as well as another
flavor dimension.*

Chutneys

Tip
Chutney is the perfect
way to add zing to a
sandwich or grilled meat.

Mint chutney

Preparation: 15 minutes

1 small pot Greek yogurt
1 bunch fresh mint
juice of 1 lime
¾ in (2 cm) piece ginger root
⅓ tsp salt

Using a food mixer, whizz together half of the
yogurt, the mint leaves, the lime juice, the
ginger (peeled and finely chopped), and the
salt.

When well blended, add the rest of the yogurt.
Refrigerate for 1 hour before serving.

*The salt will help you to chop fresh herbs
very finely, so make it the first ingredient
you put in the food mixer.*

Coconut chutney

Preparation: 15 minutes

generous 1 cup (100 g) freshly grated coconut
  or shredded coconut
1 tsp cumin seeds
1 tsp mustard seeds
1 lime
1 green chili, de-seeded
plain vegetable oil
salt

If you use shredded coconut, cover it in
lukewarm water and soak for about 1 hour.

Heat 2 tablespoons of oil in a small frying
pan and fry the cumin and mustard seeds for
5 minutes on high heat. Set to one side.

Put the fresh or shredded coconut (rehydrated
and drained), 1 tablespoon of water, the juice
of the lime, the chopped green chili, and
⅓ teaspoon of salt into a food mixer.

Blend until smooth and add the fried mixture
(oil, cumin, and mustard seeds). Whizz again
briefly to mix in the spices.

Tamarind chutney

Preparation: 20 minutes
Cooking time: 15 minutes

1 small packet of tamarind paste (5½ oz / 150 g)
1 tbsp ground coriander
1 tsp ground cumin
1 tsp chili powder
2 tbsp cane sugar
½ tsp salt

Dissolve the tamarind paste in a generous
¾ cup (200 ml) of lukewarm water for
15 minutes, then strain the thick liquid.

Bring the tamarind liquid to the boil in a pan
with all the spices, the sugar, and salt.

Thicken for 15 minutes on low heat, and pour
into a completely dry jar. Seal and store in the
refrigerator once it has cooled.

Mango chutney

Preparation: 15 minutes
Cooking time: 45 minutes

1 mango
1 tsp mustard seeds
2 tbsp superfine sugar
2 tbsp honey
¾ in (2 cm) piece ginger root
½ tsp chili powder
2 tbsp vinegar
vegetable oil
¼ tsp salt

Revise the rest of the column to read as
follows: Peel the mango and cut the flesh into
small cubes.

Fry the mustard seeds in the oil until they pop.
Avoid burning them. Add the mango cubes,
sugar, honey, grated ginger, chili, and salt.
Cover and simmer on low heat for 20
minutes until thickened, keeping an eye on it.

Add the vinegar, and simmer, uncovered, for
20 minutes. Leave to cool. Store in the fridge.

Cilantro chutney

Preparation: 15 minutes

1 bunch cilantro
1 lime
1 green chili
2 garlic cloves and 1 piece ginger root, approx.
    1 in / 3 cm (or 1 tsp garlic and ginger paste, see
    recipe on p. 26)
1 tbsp white sesame seeds
3 tbsp vegetable oil
1 tsp sugar
½ tsp salt

Peel the garlic cloves and remove any green
central shoots. Peel the ginger and chop it
coarsely.

De-seed the chili and remove the stem end.
Wash the fresh cilantro. Squeeze the juice
from the lime. Put all the ingredients in a food
mixer. Blend until smooth.

Store in the refrigerator.

Ingredients for 1 x 16 oz (500 ml) jar

Preparation: 15 minutes
Cooking time: 10 minutes

generous 1 lb (500 g) mixed
  vegetables: choose your
  own favorites, e.g. shallots,
  carrots, green mango, chili,
  fresh ginger
2 tbsp yellow mustard
  seeds, crushed
1 tbsp fenugreek seeds
⅔ cup (150 ml) white wine
  vinegar
1 tbsp vegetable oil
salt

Pickles

**Originally an Anglo-Saxon invention, pickles
(crunchy vegetables in vinegar) are an integral
part of an Indian meal. The vinegar gives these
mixtures of crunchy vegetables and spices a long
shelf life. Served with main dishes, their hint of
acidity whets the tastebuds.**

Cut the vegetables into strips or rounds. Cut the shallots
in half. Put them all in a bowl.

Fry the mustard and fenugreek seeds in the oil until they
start to brown, and pour them over the vegetables. Mix
well and season with salt. Transfer to a glass jar with a lid.

Bring the vinegar to the boil with ⅔ cup (150 ml) of water.
Pour the mixture over the raw vegetables and leave to
cool.

Seal the jar and refrigerate for at least 3 days before
eating the pickle.

The pickles will keep for 2–3 months in the refrigerator.

Chapatis

Preparation: 30 minutes
Resting time: 1 hour
Cooking time: 10 minutes
per chapati

Ingredients to make 6

⅔–generous ¾ cup (150–200 ml) lukewarm water
2 cups (300 g) whole wheat flour or atta flour (from specialist grocers)
3 tbsp olive oil
ghee or butter
½ tsp salt

These little flatbreads made with atta (or whole wheat) flour have the same status in India as the baguette has in France. The women make them once a week and keep them fresh in a damp cloth.

For the dough, mix the salt and ⅔ cup (150 ml) of water in a bowl. In another mixing bowl, combine the sifted flour and olive oil. Gradually add the salted water to the dough, mixing well.

Knead the dough for about 10 minutes until it is firm and elastic, cover the bowl with a damp cloth, and leave to rest for 1 hour.

Now divide the dough into 6 little balls. Roll them out into very thin circles, about as thick as a coin, and 8 in (20 cm) in diameter.

Heat a frying pan with a flat base and place the first chapati in it. Cook on medium heat for 5 minutes. When bubbles form, gently flatten them with a fork. Turn the chapati over and cook for 5 minutes on the other side. Spread a knob of butter or ghee over the chapati. Repeat the process for the rest of the chapatis.

As you make the 6 chapatis, place them one by one on a plate covered with aluminum foil and keep them warm in a very cool oven (100–120 °F / 40–50 °C).
If you plan to keep the chapatis for a few days (5 days maximum), wrap them in a damp cloth to stop them drying and reheat them in the oven before serving.

For info

Indian breads take many and varied forms, most of them round and flat, made with leavened or non-leavened flour—which may be white, whole wheat, Indian, etc.

Preparation: 40 minutes
Resting time: 1–2 hours
Cooking time: 10 minutes
per naan

Ingredients for 6 naan

3⅓ cups (500 g) wheat flour
1 tsp sugar
4½ oz (125 g) pot natural
  yogurt (Greek or creamy)
2 tsp (8 g) fresh baker's
  yeast
¾ cup (180 ml) water
ghee or butter
4 tbsp vegetable oil
1 tsp salt

Naan

Naans are flatbreads made with white flour and leavened dough (i.e. containing yeast). As they are more complicated and take longer to make than chapatis (involving more significant kneading and rising time), they tend to be made for special occasions only (weddings, birthdays, etc).

For the dough: combine the flour, salt, and sugar. Make a well in the middle and add the oil, yogurt, yeast, and half of the water.

Knead, using the dough hook of a food mixer or your hands, for about 15–20 minutes. The dough should become soft, and come away easily from the sides of the bowl.

Gradually add the rest of the water, kneading it until the dough is smooth. Adjust the amount of water or flour until you have the right consistency: soft dough that does not stick to the bowl.

Cover the dough with a cloth and leave it to rest and rise in a dry, warm place. The yeast action will help the dough to double or even triple in size.

After 1–2 hours, divide the dough into 6 balls the size of a tangerine and place them on a floured work surface.

Roll out the dough pieces in turn, shaping them into circles approximately 10 in (25 cm) in diameter.

If you do not have a tandoori oven, use a large, flat-bottomed frying pan with a lid.

Heat the pan, place the naan in it, cover with the lid, and turn the naan after 5 minutes.

Put a knob of ghee or butter on top of the naan. Repeat the process for the other naans and serve immediately.

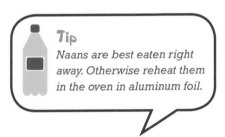

Tip
Naans are best eaten right away. Otherwise reheat them in the oven in aluminum foil.

41

Preparation: 1 hour
Resting time: 1–2 hours
Cooking time: 10 minutes
per naan

3⅓ cups (500 g) wheat flour
1 tsp sugar
4½ oz (125 g) pot natural
  yogurt (Greek or creamy)
2 tsp (8 g) fresh baker's
  yeast
¾ cup (180 ml) water
9 wedges processed cheese,
  mashed with a fork
ghee or butter
4 tbsp vegetable oil
1 tsp salt

Cheese naan

Naans made with cheese are traditionally stuffed with paneer (see p. 29), but it is now common in the West to find them made with processed cheese. No-one in India would ever dream of eating naan made with this type of cheese, but it is a way of accommodating Western tastes.

Make the naan dough (see p. 40). Divide the dough, forming 6 balls the size of a tangerine.

To stuff the naan with the cheese, make a little hole in the middle of each dough ball. Insert a large tablespoon of cheese, and seal the dough completely round the cheese to reconstitute the balls.

Flatten the dough balls into circles approximately 8 in (20 cm) diameter, making sure you do not break through the dough.

If you do not have a tandoori oven, use a large, flat-bottomed frying pan with a lid.

Heat the pan, place the naan in it, cover with the lid, and turn the naan after 5 minutes.

Put a knob of ghee or butter on top of the naan. Repeat the process for the other naans, and serve immediately.

Preparation: 45 minutes
Resting time: 1 hour
Cooking time: 10 minutes
per paratha

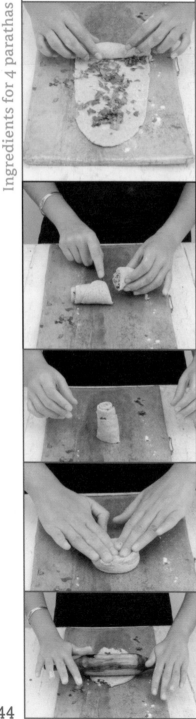

Paratha with cilantro
Kothmir paratha

Parathas are chapatis made in a slightly different way. More than just a simple flatbread, the dough mixture and process give them a flaky texture.

For the chapati dough
1⅓ cups (200 g) whole wheat or atta flour (from specialist grocers)
7 tbsp (100 ml) lukewarm water
2 tbsp vegetable oil or melted ghee
½ tsp salt

For the filling
1 tbsp garlic paste (see recipe on p. 26)
5–6 sprigs cilantro
2 tbsp (30 g) unsalted butter or melted ghee

Make the chapati dough (see p. 38, paragraphs 1 and 2). Prepare the parathas: divide the dough into 2 balls. Roll out each piece of dough very thinly into a large rectangle, about the thickness of a coin. Dust the work surface and dough pieces with flour as required.

Brush each piece of the dough with butter or melted ghee, then spread the garlic paste on it and sprinkle with chopped cilantro. Roll the dough into a snail shape and cut it in half to make 2 rolls. Carefully flatten the first dough roll into a circle about 6 in (15 cm) in diameter, and then repeat for the second one.

Pre-heat a flat-bottomed frying pan or tawa (chapati pan) and place the paratha in it. Turn it over after 5 minutes, when the paratha begins to smoke slightly. Brush with butter or ghee and cook on the other side for 5 minutes.

Put the parathas on a plate and cover with a sheet of aluminum foil to keep them warm. Serve hot.

Raita

Raita
with spinach

Raita
with cucumber and mint

Raita
with mango and cilantro

Raita
with tomato and ginger

Raita

Ingredients to serve 4

Raita is a small side dish made with whole milk yogurt and vegetables, or sometimes fruit. With just a hint of spice, it soothes the palate when eating spicy dishes. It can also be served as a salad to accompany grilled meat.

Raita with spinach

Preparation: 15 minutes
Cooking time: 5 minutes

1 garlic clove
1 tsp (5 g) butter (or ghee)
1 handful freshly chopped spinach
2 small pots Greek yogurt
salt

Fry the chopped garlic in the butter or ghee for 5 minutes on medium heat. Add the freshly chopped spinach and wilt it for a few minutes. Season with salt, and leave to cool.

When the spinach has cooled down, gently combine it with the yogurt. Serve at room temperature.

Raita with cucumber and mint

Preparation: 15 minutes

½ cucumber
2 small pots Greek yogurt
1 tbsp squeezed lime juice
5–6 sprigs mint
1 pinch ground cumin
salt

Peel the cucumber, remove the seeds, and grate it coarsely. Season with salt, and set to one side.

Whisk the yogurt with the lime juice and cumin until it froths. Combine it with the grated cucumber and finely chopped mint.

Refrigerate for 1 hour before serving.

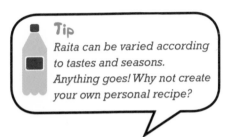

Tip

Raita can be varied according to tastes and seasons. Anything goes! Why not create your own personal recipe?

Raita with mango and cilantro

Preparation: 15 minutes

2 small pots Greek yogurt
1 tbsp squeezed lime juice
½ ripe mango, still slightly firm
5–6 sprigs cilantro
1 small piece ginger root
salt

Whisk the yogurt with the lime juice and salt until it froths. Set to one side.

Peel the mango and cut it into ⅓ in (1 cm) cubes. Add them to the whisked yogurt, along with the chopped cilantro and ginger, peeled and finely grated.

Refrigerate for 1 hour before serving.

Raita with tomato and ginger

Preparation: 15 minutes

2 small pots Greek yogurt
1 tbsp squeezed lime juice
1 tomato
1 red onion or 3–4 small shallots
a few cilantro leaves
1 small piece ginger root
salt

Whisk the yogurt with the lime juice and salt. Set to one side.

Blanch the tomato (soak briefly in boiling water and remove the skin), remove the seeds, and dice it. Chop the onion very finely, chop the cilantro, and finely grate the ginger.

Combine all the ingredients with the whisked yogurt and refrigerate for at least 1 hour.

Thali

The thali represents the classic Indian meal. Each container has the amounts required for a balanced diet, namely a small portion of meat or fish weighing about 4 oz (100 g)—for a vegetarian thali this would be replaced by a vegetable or portion of paneer—a portion of potato, a portion of green vegetables (essential), a portion of lentils (dahl), a raita, a chutney, and a seasonal raw vegetable salad or pickles, as well as something sweet. Rice (often white), a chapatti, and a papadum are found in the middle of the thali.

Thali suggestion 1
Potato, cauliflower, and pea curry (p. 118)
Yellow lentil korma (p. 112)
Mango chutney (p. 35)
Spinach with paneer (p. 120)
Pickled onions (p. 36)
Raita with tomato and ginger (p. 49)
Banana halva (p. 141)

Thali suggestion 2
Tamarind chutney (p. 35)
Fried okra (p. 125)
Mashed eggplant curry (p. 117)
Creamy green lentil curry (p. 112)
Tandoori chicken (p. 82)
Ginger pickles (p. 36)
Almond bonbons (p. 137)

Lunch box

The "lunch box," or "dabba," is an institution in India, especially in the big cities. In the morning, a woman cooks for her husband, and then a delivery worker picks up the box and takes it to his place of work. It always contains a tier for bread or rice, one for vegetables, and one for dahl. As dessert does not really exist in India as such, people tend to snack on something sweet (a mitha) in the afternoon.

Lunch box suggestion 1
Vegetable balls with paneer and creamy sauce (p. 122)
Cardamom rice (p. 20)
Raita with mango and coriander (p. 49)

Lunch box suggestion 2
Fried okra (p. 125)
Tandoori chicken (p. 82)
Naan (p. 40)

Lunch box suggestion 3
Potato, cauliflower, and pea curry (p. 118)
Yellow lentil curry (p. 112)
Chapatis (p. 38)

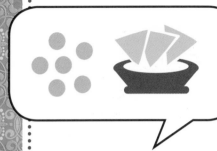

Snacking

This section gives a good idea of the "street food" approach in India: eating informally in the street at any time of night or day, whether it is something sweet or savory, or a drink … There are no set rules when it comes to the Indian nation's passion for snacking!

Samosas

Samosas are the symbol of street food in India. They are eaten countrywide and on every street, in any dhaba (roadside restaurant), or at the tiniest kiosk ... The most common version of samosa is filled with dry potato curry, and it is also the most nutritious. Two different forms of pastry are given here: the ready-made version is modern, while the kneaded one is more traditional. The choice is up to you! I also give you the option of two folding methods: the traditional one (step-by-step, pp. 57–58) and the faster version (step-by-step, p. 56).

Traditional samosa dough

Preparation: 15 minutes
Resting time: 30 minutes

1¾ cups (250 g) all-purpose flour
2 tbsp creamy natural yogurt
2 tbsp sunflower oil
½ tsp salt

Combine the flour and salt, and form a well in the middle. Add the yogurt and oil and mix well.

Add the water in stages, kneading the dough into a smooth ball. Leave to rest for 30 minutes.

Roll the dough out thinly. Cut it into 4 in (10 cm) circles with a pastry cutter.

Samosas with ready-made pastry

6 sheets ready-made pastry (such as filo or spring roll pastry)
1 tbsp (10 g) all-purpose flour
2 tbsp water
oil for frying

Cut the pastry sheets in half to make 12 rectangles. Fold each of these in half, making 12 strips.

Mix the flour and water to make a paste. Lay the first strip horizontally in front of you and place a tablespoon of filling of your choice on the left-hand side.

Fold over in triangles, pressing the corners down firmly. When you come to the last fold, spread on some of the flour paste to seal the end of the strip.

Fry the samosas in ¾ in (2 cm) of oil (hot but not smoking) for 3 minutes on each side on medium heat, turning occasionally as they cook. They should be golden in color.

Drain on kitchen paper and serve immediately.

Vegetable samosas
Aloo samosa

Preparation: 15 minutes
Cooking time: 10 minutes

Ingredients for 8 samosas

For the dough
See ingredients on p. 56

For the filling
generous 1 lb (500 g)
   potatoes
5½ oz (150 g) carrots
5½ oz (150 g) frozen peas
1 inch (3 cm) piece fresh
   ginger root
4–5 sprigs freshly chopped
   cilantro leaves
1 tsp mustard seeds
1 tsp cumin seeds
juice of 1 lime for serving
vegetable oil

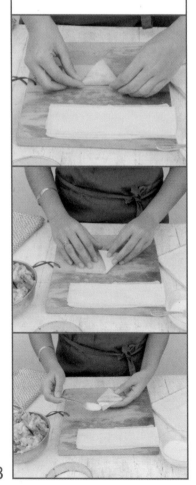

Make traditional samosa dough following the recipe on page 56.

Peel the carrots and potatoes, and then dice them all. Cook for 10 minutes in boiling water. Peel and grate the ginger, then fry it in a pan with 1 tablespoon of oil for 5 minutes on medium heat.

Add the mustard seeds, then the cumin, and brown for 1–2 minutes. De-glaze with some water. When the water has evaporated again, add the drained vegetables and peas, crushing them all coarsely. Remove the pan from the stovetop and add the freshly chopped cilantro.

Put a teaspoon of filling in the middle of each dough circle. Pull the edges up into the center, forming 3 edges, and seal it all well. Fry the samosas in ¾ in (2 cm) of oil (hot but not smoking) for 3 minutes on each side on medium heat, turning occasionally as they cook. They should be golden in color. Serve with some lime juice or cilantro chutney (recipe on p. 35).

More ideas for fillings
1/ Beef and peas: brown ⅔ cup (150 g) ground beef with 1 chopped onion, ⅓ in (1 cm) piece of fresh ginger, grated, and 1 crushed garlic clove for 10 minutes on medium heat. Remove the pan from the stovetop, and add some freshly chopped cilantro and peas.

2/ Coconut chicken: mix together 5½ oz (150 g) leftover roast chicken with a pinch of curry powder and generous ¾ cup (200 ml) of coconut milk, 1 cooked mashed potato, and 5 fresh cilantro leaves for 5 minutes on medium heat.

3/ Zucchini: brown 1 diced zucchini in 1 tablespoon of vegetable oil with 1 tablespoon of cumin seeds and a pinch of ground turmeric for 10 minutes on medium heat.

Papadums

Papadums, also known as papads or poppadums, are an Indian snack—similar to our Western potato chips. They come in various shapes (round or oblong) and different flavors (spicy, with cumin, or pepper). They are thin, crispy flatbreads made from flour—chickpea, lentil, or rice, or a mixture of these. Various spices, chilis, and aromatic flavors may be added as well. Papadums are usually bought in dried form, and cooked at the last minute. They are served crispy. Toppings can also be added for a fresh, crunchy, and colorful starter!

Mini-papads with pepper

Spicy chili papad

To cook papadums, all of them (except rice-based ones) can be grilled on an open flame, deep-fried, or dry-fried in a pan. A word of warning: papadums do not tolerate moisture; it makes them soggy.

Small plain papads

Long, spoon-shape papads

Cumin papads

Rice papads

Preparation: 10 minutes
Cooking time: 10 minutes

Ingredients for 4 papads with topping

4 cumin-flavor papadums
1 tomato
4 shallots
4–5 sprigs fresh cilantro
  leaves
1 green chili

Papadum with topping
Masala salad papad

These wafer-thin chips made with chickpea or lentil flour are bought ready-made and cooked dry in a frying pan.

Peel and chop the shallots. Chop the tomatoes and remove the seeds. Chop the cilantro. Chop the chili and remove the seeds.

Cook the papadums individually in a hot frying pan for 3 minutes on each side, flattening them with a spatula so they remain flat and cook evenly.

When you are ready to serve, top with tomato, shallots, and cilantro. Sprinkle with chili.

Serve with your favorite chutney (see recipes on pp. 34–35).

Tip
Cook the papads for a few seconds in the microwave. While this is not as authentic, you will save on calories.

Preparation: 15 minutes
Resting time: 1 hour
Cooking time: 5 minutes

Ingredients to serve 4

1 tbsp cornstarch
1 tbsp all-purpose flour
1 tsp tandoori spices
14 oz (400 g) fresh paneer,
  cut into approx. 1 in / 3 cm
  cubes (see recipe on p. 29)
juice of 1 lime
vegetable oil
salt

Fried paneer
Paneer tikka

In a small bowl, combine the cornstarch, flour, spices, and a pinch of salt.

Mix in 5 tablespoons of water and soak the paneer cubes in this paste, coating well. Refrigerate for 1 hour.

Heat ⅓ in (1 cm) vegetable oil in a frying pan (it should be hot, but not smoking).

Fry the paneer in the hot oil until golden in color (about 5 minutes on each side), then drain on kitchen paper. Serve immediately, drizzled with lime juice.

You can make your own tandoori spice mix with 1 teaspoon of ground coriander, 1 teaspoon of ground cumin, and ½ teaspoon of turmeric (add some red food coloring if you like).

Tip
Tandoori spice mixes may be slightly salty already, so taste before seasoning.

Cashew nuts with garam masala

Masala kaju

Dry-roast the cashew nuts on medium heat for 5 minutes in a very hot (but not smoking) frying pan. Dust with the spices and mix well, ensuring all the nuts are coated. Season with salt and serve.

Preparation: 2 minutes
Cooking time: 5 minutes

1⅓ cups (200 g) cashew nuts, raw and unsalted
1 tbsp garam masala
1 pinch chili powder
1 pinch fine salt

Tip
Try using different nuts, such as almonds and hazelnuts, and your favorite spices (cumin, paprika, etc).

Preparation: 20 minutes
Resting time: 2 hours
30 minutes
Cooking time: 10 minutes

¾ cup (150 g) red lentils
1 pinch turmeric
generous pinch red chili
   powder
1 garlic clove, any central
   green shoot removed
1 red onion
1 dozen sprigs fresh cilantro
1 tsp cumin seeds
2 tbsp chickpea flour
¾ in (2 cm) vegetable
   shortening
salt

Spicy lentil fritters

Masala vadai

Masala vadai is an excellent example of Indian street food. It is served for breakfast in some regions and is equally popular as a snack with a very sweet cup of chai in the afternoon.

Rinse the lentils and soak them in a large bowl of cold water for 2 hours. Drain, then whizz them in a food mixer with the turmeric, chili powder, garlic clove, onion cut into 8 pieces, cilantro with stalks, and a generous pinch of salt. The mixture should be combined well, but not completely smooth, and slightly moist. Mix in the cumin seeds and chickpea flour. Leave to rest for 30 minutes at room temperature.

Heat the vegetable shortening in a frying pan (it should be hot, but not smoking). Using 2 tablespoons or your hands, shape the mixture into small balls (1 small tablespoon per fritter) and drop them carefully into the hot oil. Fry for 5 minutes on each side until golden. Serve with your raita of choice (see recipe on p. 48).

For an evening buffet, make little balls ¾ in (2 cm) in diameter—using a melon baller, for instance— and serve on cocktail sticks.

Spicy eggplant fries

Baingan brinjal

Cut the eggplants into chunky fries and coat lightly with flour.

Heat the vegetable shortening (it should be hot, but not smoking) in a frying pan. Drop the eggplant fries into the pan and fry until golden in color (approximately 5 minutes on each side). Drain on kitchen paper.

Sprinkle with salt and paprika, and serve immediately.

You can also try using sweet potato or zucchini.

Preparation: 5 minutes
Cooking time: 10 minutes

3–4 small eggplants, long, firm, and glossy (or 1 large one)
2 tbsp all-purpose flour
⅓ in (1 cm) vegetable shortening
sweet paprika
salt

Ingredients to serve 4

Mixed vegetable fritters
Pakora

For the batter: combine the flour and all the spices.
Season with salt. Gradually add warm water (about
1 cup / 250 ml) until the batter is smooth and not too thick.

Prepare the vegetables: cut them all into little sticks or
rounds approximately 2 in (5 cm) across.

Dip the vegetables in the batter in batches, using 2 forks
to lift them out. Shake off any excess batter.

Heat the vegetable shortening (it should be hot, but not
smoking) in a frying pan. Drop the vegetables carefully
into the hot oil. Fry the pakora until golden in color all
over, turning frequently (about 5 minutes each side).
Drain on kitchen paper.

Serve immediately with your favorite raita (see recipes on
pp. 48–49).

Preparation: 15 minutes
Cooking time: 10 minutes

1¾ cups (250 g) chickpea
  flour
1 tsp ground cumin
1 tsp garam masala
1 tsp paprika or chili powder
1 small eggplant
1 red onion
1 zucchini
¼ cauliflower
⅓ in (1 cm) vegetable
  shortening
salt

Ingredients to serve 4

73

Meat and fish

Meat forms part of the Indian diet: 60 percent of Indian people eat it, but in small quantities. Fish and shellfish are found almost exclusively near the coastline and in large cities such as Goa and Madras.

Preparation: 15 minutes
Resting time: 2–3 hours
Cooking time: 45 minutes

generous 1 lb (500 g)
  chicken portions: legs,
  thighs, drumsticks, etc.
2 small pots natural yogurt
  (set or creamy)
juice of 1 lime
½ tsp turmeric
6 garlic cloves (any central
  green shoots removed)
1 tsp ginger paste (see
  recipe on p. 26)
4–5 curry leaves
6 cardamom pods
1 cinnamon stick
4 cloves
4–5 sprigs fresh cilantro
3 onions, preferably red
4 tbsp vegetable oil

Chicken with yogurt, garlic, and turmeric

Dahi chicken curry

Trim the chicken pieces: remove the skin and excess fat, and make slits in the flesh with a sharp knife.

Make the yogurt marinade: in a shallow bowl, thoroughly combine the yogurt, lime juice, 2 tablespoons of vegetable oil, turmeric, crushed garlic cloves, and the ginger paste. Coat the chicken all over with the mixture and leave to rest for 2–3 hours.

Heat the remaining 2 tablespoons of oil and fry the curry leaves, cardamom pods, cinnamon stick, cloves, and finely chopped onions for 10 minutes on medium heat until lightly browned, stirring all the time.

Add the chicken and the yogurt from the marinade, searing the chicken quickly for 5 minutes on medium heat. Add 7 tablespoons (100 ml) of water, cover the pan, and simmer on low heat for 25–30 minutes.

Serve sprinkled with freshly chopped cilantro, a chapati (see recipe on p. 38), and mint chutney (see recipe on p. 34).

Lamb kebabs with ginger and cilantro

Preparation: 10 minutes
Resting time: 1 hour to overnight
Cooking time: 10–12 minutes

1 green chili (optional)
1 tbsp ginger paste (see recipe on p. 26)
1 tsp garam masala
½ bunch fresh cilantro
generous 1 lb (500 g) leg of lamb, de-boned
1 tbsp vegetable oil

Ingredients to serve 4

Remove the seeds and stem end of the chili.

Whizz the ginger paste, garam masala, cilantro, green chili, and a small amount of oil in a food mixer.

Dice the lamb into 1–1½ in (3–4 cm) cubes. Dip them in the spice mix, coating them well, and marinate at room temperature for 1–2 hours (ideally overnight), covered in plastic wrap.

When the meat has marinated, thread the cubes onto skewers and grill for 10–12 minutes on each side, either on a barbecue or an oven grill pre-heated to 425 °F (220 °C).

Serve with some pickles (p. 36), chutney (pp. 34–35), or your favorite raita (pp. 48–49).

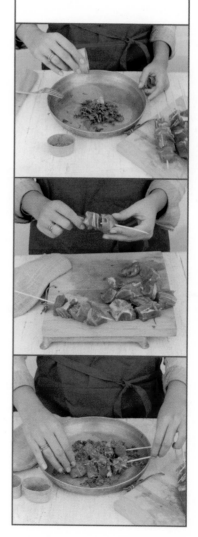

Preparation: 15 minutes
Resting time: 1–2 hours
Cooking time: 35–40 minutes

Ingredients to serve 4

1 small pot whole milk natural yogurt
1 tbsp ground almonds
1 tbsp garlic and ginger paste (see recipe on p. 26)
spices: ½ tsp paprika,
 ¼ tsp ground cinnamon,
 ¼ tsp chili powder,
 4 cardamom pods,
 2 cloves, 1 tsp ground coriander
1 lb (450 g) chicken breasts
2 tbsp (30 g) butter
1 onion
1 green chili, de-seeded
1 tsp ground fenugreek leaves
chili2 x 5 oz (140 g) cans concentrated tomato paste
7 tbsp (100 ml) passata
liquid honey
juice of 1 lime
7 tbsp (100 ml) light cream
a few chopped, toasted cashew nuts
a few cilantro leaves for garnish
2 tbsp vegetable oil
salt

Butter chicken
Mugh makhani

In a large shallow dish, combine the yogurt, oil, ground almonds, half of the garlic and ginger paste, paprika, cinnamon, and chili powder. Dip the chicken pieces in this marinade, coating them well. Leave to marinade for 1–2 hours.

Pre-heat the oven to 410 °F (210 °C).

Transfer the chicken pieces to an ovenproof dish. Roast in the oven for 15–20 minutes, turning them halfway through the cooking time.

Meanwhile make the butter sauce. Melt the butter in a frying pan on low heat. Add the rest of the garlic and ginger paste, cardamom pods, cloves, onion, and finely chopped green chili. Fry the mixture for 10 minutes on medium heat.

Add the ground coriander and fenugreek leaves, mixing well. Then add the tomato paste, passata, honey, and 7 tablespoons (100 ml) of water. Simmer for 10 minutes on low heat.

When ready to serve, squeeze some lime juice over the sauce and mix in the cream. Serve the chicken coated in the creamy sauce, sprinkled with cashew nuts and cilantro.

Preparation: 10 minutes
Resting time: 2 hours
Cooking time: 25 minutes

Ingredients to serve 4

- 1 small pot whole milk natural yogurt
- 1 tsp ground coriander
- 1 tsp ground cumin
- ½ tsp ground turmeric
- 1 tbsp garlic and ginger paste (see recipe on p. 26)
- 1 tsp concentrated tomato paste
- juice of 1 lime
- 2–3 sprigs fresh cilantro
- 4 chicken fillets, or other cuts if you prefer
- 1 tbsp vegetable oil
- salt

Tandoori chicken
Murgh tandoori

The yogurt marinade will act as the base for your grilled meat dishes. It goes well with all types of white meat, and even lamb. Food coloring gives it the familiar red color.

Make the marinade. In a large dish, combine the yogurt with the spices, garlic and ginger paste, tomato paste, lime juice, vegetable oil, and finely chopped cilantro.

Dip the chicken pieces in this marinade, coating them well, and refrigerate for at least 2 hours.

Pre-heat the oven to 410 °F (210 °C).

Transfer the chicken to an ovenproof dish (discard the excess marinade).

Season the chicken with salt to taste and roast it in the oven for 25 minutes, turning halfway through the cooking time (or you can barbecue it). Serve immediately with mint chutney (see recipe on p. 34).

There are hundreds of recipes for tandoori chicken. The basis is a mixture of spices and yogurt, which helps to tenderize the chicken.

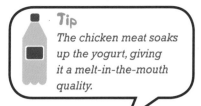

Tip
The chicken meat soaks up the yogurt, giving it a melt-in-the-mouth quality.

Lamb curry with cinnamon

Rogan josh

Peel and crush the garlic. Peel and grate the ginger.

Sweat the onions with 1 tablespoon of oil and a pinch of salt in a casserole for 10 minutes on medium heat. Set to one side.

Cut the lamb joint into large, even chunks approximately 1 in (3 cm) square. Brown them in the casserole with 1 tablespoon of oil, the garlic, and the ginger for 10 minutes on medium heat.

While the meat is browning, peel and de-seed the tomatoes. Chop them coarsely and set to one side.

When the lamb is well browned, add the turmeric, ground coriander, cardamom, and cinnamon, stirring well. Fry for 5 minutes on medium heat.

Add the cooked onions, passata, and ⅔ cup (150 ml) of water. Simmer on low heat for 25 minutes. Add the chopped tomatoes and simmer for another 25 minutes.

Serve immediately with a chapati (see recipe on p. 38).

Serve immediately with a chapati (see recipe on p. 38).

Preparation: 20 minutes
Cooking time: 1 hour
15 minutes

2 garlic cloves
1 in (3 cm) piece ginger root
3 red onions
generous 1 lb (500 g) leg of lamb
2 tomatoes
½ tsp turmeric
1 tsp ground coriander
5 cardamom pods
2 cinnamon sticks or ½ tsp ground cinnamon
⅔ cup (150 ml) passata
vegetable oil
salt

Ingredients to serve 4

Chicken korma
Murgh korma

Preparation: 20 minutes
Resting time: 1–2 hours
Cooking time: 30 minutes

Ingredients to serve 4

- 2 tbsp (20 g) blanched almonds, unsalted
- 2 tbsp (20 g) cashew nuts, unsalted and untoasted
- 14 oz (400 g) chicken breast, free-range
- 1 small pot creamy natural yogurt
- ½ tsp turmeric
- juice of ½ lime
- 1 bay leaf
- 1 star anise
- 1 tsp garlic paste (see recipe on p. 26)
- 1 tsp ginger paste (see recipe on p. 26)
- 1 tbsp ground coriander
- 3 green cardamom pods
- 1 pinch red chili powder
- 1 small red onion
- 1 tbsp ghee
- scant 1 tablespoon of cashew nuts, flaked almonds, or pistachios for garnish
- chili
- 2 tbsp vegetable oil
- salt

Whizz the almonds and cashew nuts into a smooth cream with 7 tablespoons (100 ml) of water. Set to one side.

Cut the chicken into approximately ¾ in (2 cm) cubes. In a bowl, combine 1 tablespoon of yogurt with the turmeric and lime juice. Add the chicken, mix well, and refrigerate for 1–2 hours.

Heat 1 tablespoon of oil in a frying pan. Brown the chicken pieces for 5 minutes on high heat. Transfer them to a dish and set to one side.

Add 1 tablespoon of oil to the same pan and fry the bay leaf, star anise, garlic and ginger pastes, ground coriander, cardamom, and chili powder for 10 minutes on high heat, stirring all the time. Add 1 small glass of water and the nut cream, stir well, and simmer gently for 10 minutes.

Add the chicken and the rest of the yogurt, season with salt, and cook on low heat for a further 10 minutes. Add some water if the sauce becomes too thick.

Meanwhile, brown the finely chopped red onion in 1 tablespoon of ghee for 10 minutes on medium heat. Set to one side on some paper towels.

Dry-roast some flaked almonds, blanched pistachios, or cashew nuts in a small pan. Serve the chicken sprinkled with nuts and onions, accompanied by Basmati rice.

Chicken tikka
Murgh tikka masala

Ingredients to serve 4

1 lb (450 g) chicken
   breasts
1 small pot whole milk
   natural yogurt
spices: 1 tsp ground
   coriander, 2 small dried
   red chilis (optional),
   4 cardamom pods,
   2 cloves, 2 bay leaves,
   1 tbsp garam masala
1 red onion
1 tbsp garlic and ginger
   paste (see recipe on
   p. 26)
4–5 sprigs cilantro
1 can chopped tomatoes
   (14 oz / 400 ml)
1 green chili
1 mild red chili or
1 small red bell pepper
juice of 1 lime
3 tbsp vegetable oil
salt

Dice the chicken into ¾ in (2 cm) cubes.

In a large dish, combine the yogurt, 1 tablespoon of oil, and the ground coriander. Add the chicken, coating it well, and marinade for 1–2 hours.

Pre-heat the oven to 410 °F (210 °C).

Transfer the chicken pieces to an ovenproof dish. Roast them for 15–20 minutes, turning halfway through the cooking time. Set to one side.

Meanwhile, make the sauce. In a frying pan containing 2 tablespoons of oil, sweat the chopped onion, dried chilis, cardamom, cloves, and bay leaf for 10 minutes on medium heat. Mix well and add the garlic and ginger paste, garam masala, and some salt. Cook on medium heat for 5 minutes, stirring all the time. Add a small glass of water (½ cup / 120 ml) and reduce the liquid. Add the chopped tomatoes. Stir well and cook the sauce on medium heat for 10 minutes to thicken it.

De-seed the green chili and red chili (or bell pepper). Cut them into ¾ in (2 cm) cubes, and add them to the sauce mix together with the cooked chicken. To serve, squeeze some lime juice over the sauce and sprinkle with chopped cilantro.

You can replace the sauce with 4 tablespoons of curry paste (see recipe on p. 25). If you do this, return to the recipe for the final paragraph.

Lamb vindaloo
Gosth vindaloo

Preparation: 15 minutes
Resting time: 3 hours minimum, ideally overnight
Cooking time: 50 minutes

3 small dried red chilis
7 tablespoons (100 ml) coconut milk
1 tsp mustard seeds
1 tsp garam masala
1 tbsp garlic paste
1 tbsp ginger paste
1 small tin concentrated tomato paste
generous 1 lb (500 g) leg of lamb, de-boned
1 red onion
1 small red bell pepper
vegetable oil
salt

In a large dish, soak the dried chilis in the coconut milk together with the mustard seeds, garam masala, garlic and ginger pastes, and tomato paste for 30 minutes. Then whizz the mixture in a food mixer.

Cut the lamb into chunks and soak it in this marinade for at least 3 hours, ideally overnight.

Drain the lamb chunks, reserving the marinade. Heat 2 tablespoons of oil in a frying pan until very hot, and sear the marinated lamb for 5–7 minutes on high heat.

Add 7 tablespoons (100 ml) of water and ¼ teaspoon of salt to the marinade.

Put the red onion and chopped bell pepper in the frying pan and pour in the marinade. Cover and cook for 45 minutes on medium heat, checking that the meat does not stick to the pan. Add some more water if required as it cooks.

For info
Of all the curries, I go for very hot, spicy ones!

Tikka masala fish

Preparation: 20 minutes
Resting time: 15 minutes
Cooking time: 25 minutes

Ingredients to serve 4

1⅓ tbsp (20 g) tamarind paste
4 very ripe tomatoes or 1 small can chopped tomatoes
2 onions
2 mild green chilis or 1 small green bell pepper
1 tbsp garlic and ginger paste (see recipe on p. 26)
1 tsp ground coriander
½ tsp chili powder
¼ tsp turmeric
1 tsp garam masala
1 small tin concentrated tomato paste
2 tbsp all-purpose flour
1 tbsp (15 g) butter or ghee
4 hake loin, skin on, cut into chunks
4–5 sprigs fresh cilantro
vegetable oil
salt

Soak the tamarind paste for 15 minutes in a generous ¾ cup (200 ml) of lukewarm water. Strain, and reserve the juice.

If using fresh tomatoes, plunge them into boiling water for a few minutes, then peel and de-seed them. Whizz the tomatoes into a purée and set to one side.

Make the sauce. Heat 2 tablespoons of vegetable oil in a frying pan. Add the very finely chopped onions and the green chilis or bell pepper, de-seeded and finely diced. Cook on high heat for 4–5 minutes, stirring all the time.

Add the garlic and ginger paste, the ground spices (coriander, chili, turmeric, garam masala), ¼ teaspoon of salt, tomato paste, and tamarind juice. Reduce the liquid until it is the consistency of a paste, and add the tomatoes. Cover and simmer gently for 15 minutes. Set this masala sauce to one side.

Coat the fish in flour, shaking off any excess.

Meanwhile, melt the butter in a frying pan with 2 tablespoons of oil and fry the fish, skin side down first, then turn. Drain on paper towels, then serve coated with masala sauce and sprinkled with some cilantro leaves.

"Masala" (meaning "mixture") is now used to describe a sauce made with a mixture of spices.

For info

As the fish is meant to remain slightly firm, the skin is kept on while cooking to keep it intact.

Steamed fish in banana leaves
Ras chawal masala fish

If using shredded coconut, soak it for 30 minutes in hot water, then drain.

Make the tamarind juice: soak the tamarind paste in ⅔ cup (150 ml) of lukewarm water to dilute the paste; strain and reserve the juice.

Whizz all the following ingredients in a food mixer with the tamarind juice: coconut, cilantro, ginger paste, green chili, coriander, and cumin. Season with salt.

Pre-heat the oven to 320 °F (160 °C).

Meanwhile, gut and scale the fish (or ask at the fish counter to have this done), and stuff them with the coconut paste. Fix in place with 1 or 2 wooden cocktail sticks.

Arrange a few lime slices on top of the sea bass. Place each fish on a banana leaf, fold the leaf over to close on all sides, and seal in place with cocktail sticks.

Bake the parcels in the oven for 15 minutes (or 25 minutes for a large fish).

Serve with a squeeze of lime juice.

Preparation: 10 minutes
Resting time: 30 minutes
Cooking time:
15–25 minutes

⅓ cup (30 g) freshly grated or shredded coconut
1⅓ tbsp (20 g) tamarind paste
½ bunch fresh cilantro
1 tsp ginger paste (see recipe on p. 26)
1 green chili, de-seeded and chopped
1 tsp ground coriander
1 tsp ground cumin
2 sea bass, each approx. 1¼ lb (600 g) or 1 large one, 3 lb (1.3 kg) approx.
1 lime
2 banana leaves, or waxed paper
salt

Ingredients to serve 4

95

Preparation: 20 minutes
Cooking time: 40 minutes

Ingredients to serve 4

juice of 1 lime
½ tsp turmeric
11 oz (300 g) large raw
  shrimp, tail on and
  de-veined
¼ cup (20 g) freshly grated
  coconut or 7 tbsp (100 ml)
  coconut cream
2 tbsp (20 g) unsalted
  blanched almonds
1 small pot creamy natural
  yogurt
1 tsp garlic paste (see
  recipe on p. 26)
1 tsp ginger paste (see
  recipe on p. 26)
3 green cardamom pods
2 cloves
1 tsp ground coriander
1 pinch red chili powder
4–5 sprigs fresh cilantro
vegetable oil or ghee
sugar
salt

Shrimp curry with coconut
Jhinga korma masala

Make a marinade with the lime juice and ½ teaspoon of turmeric, add the raw shrimp, and refrigerate. Set to one side.

Whizz the coconut, almonds, and yogurt in a food mixer until fairly smooth. Set to one side.

Heat 2 tablespoons of oil in a large frying pan, and fry the garlic and ginger pastes, cardamom, and cloves on medium heat for 5 minutes, stirring all the time.

Add the ground coriander, chili powder, and 7 tbsp (100 ml) of water, and reduce the liquid for 10 minutes on medium heat.

Add the coconut and almond purée, cover, and simmer gently for 15 minutes. Do not allow it to boil.

Add the marinated shrimp to the sauce, season with salt, and stir well. Simmer gently for 10 minutes.

Remove the whole spices and serve sprinkled with fresh cilantro.

Tip
It is important to rinse pulses well to remove any impurities.

Rice and lentils

Rice plays a key role in complementing lentils in the Indian diet for all social classes, and especially for vegetarians. Easily digested, lentils are suitable for all types of diet and are even more nutritious when served with rice. Combining lentils and rice effectively increases the intake of proteins. Indian lentils are eaten well cooked, whole or mashed, and with or without the seed coat. They come in a variety of shapes and colors: yellow, black, red, green, whole, mashed, de-hulled, pre-washed, and in oil. The type of rice used in this section is Basmati, one of the many varieties of rice cultivated in India; it is often called "the king of rice." The long thin grains become even longer when soaked and cooked. Basmati rice improves with age! Some old, rare, and expensive types of rice may be found on sale.

Ingredients to serve 6

- 2 small pots creamy natural yogurt
- 2 tbsp garam masala
- 1 tsp garlic paste (see recipe on p. 26)
- 1 tsp ginger paste (see recipe on p. 26)
- ½ bunch fresh cilantro
- ½ bunch mint
- 2 cups (400 g) Basmati rice
- 3 red onions
- a few cashew nuts
- 2 cardamom pods, 2 bay leaves, 1 cinnamon stick, 1 star anise, 2 cloves
- 6 chicken portions, bone in (legs or thighs)
- 1 pinch saffron powder
- 7 tbsp (100 ml) warm milk
- vegetable oil
- ½ tsp salt

Hyderabadi chicken biryani

In a mixing bowl, combine the yogurt, garam masala, half of the garlic and ginger pastes, half of the chopped cilantro and mint, and 1 tablespoon of vegetable oil. Refrigerate for 2 hours.

Rinse the rice and soak it for 1–2 hours.

Fry 1 chopped onion and the cashew nuts in 2 tablespoons of oil for 5 minutes on medium heat. Set to one side.

In a casserole dish, fry the other 2 onions, chopped, in 2 tablespoons of oil with the rest of the garlic and ginger pastes, the cardamom, 1 bay leaf, cinnamon, and star anise, and ½ teaspoon of salt for 10 minutes on high heat, stirring all the time. Add the marinated chicken portions and sear for 5 minutes on each side.

Drain the rice and transfer it to a pan of cold water. Add the 2 cloves, 1 bay leaf, and 2 tablespoons of oil. Bring to the boil and cook for 10 minutes on medium heat, then drain. Set this pre-cooked rice to one side.

Soak the saffron in the warm milk. Set to one side. Now combine all 4 mixtures. Arrange the chicken pieces in the casserole dish, spoon the rice on top, then the rest of the chopped cilantro and mint, and the saffron milk. Cover with a lid and bake in the oven at 355 °F (180 °C) for 30 minutes.

When ready to serve, stir the rice and chicken well. Sprinkle with the toasted cashew nuts and fried onions. Serve piping hot.

For info

Biryani is a festive dish, often served at banquets, weddings, and other special family occasions. The Hyderabadi version uses saffron to give the rice a bright yellow color.

Saffron rice
Zafrani pulao

Prepare and cook the rice as in the instructions on page 19.

While the rice is cooking, prepare the saffron. Soak the strands in 2 tablespoons of lukewarm water. Leave to infuse.

When the rice has cooked and rested, mix 4 teaspoons of rice with the saffron water.

Mix well to spread the color evenly, and combine the saffron rice with the remaining white rice.

Serve immediately.

Tip
Saffron should be used sparingly: it is almost literally worth its weight in gold!

1⅓ cups (250 g) Basmati rice
1 pinch saffron strands
+ 1 pinch for garnish
½ tsp fine salt

Ingredients to serve 4

Ingredients to serve 4

1½ cups (300 g) Basmati
   rice
1 zucchini
1 firm tomato
1 red onion
1 garlic clove
1½ tbsp (10 g) toasted
   flaked almonds
whole spices: 3 cardamom
   pods, 2 star anise,
   1 cinnamon stick, 1 clove
½ tsp turmeric
vegetable oil
salt

Pulao rice with zucchini

Tura pulao

Rinse and drain the rice. Soak in fresh water for 30 minutes.

Meanwhile chop the zucchini, tomato, and red onion into small cubes, approximately 5 mm, on each side. Peel and crush the garlic clove.

Heat 2 tablespoons of oil in a pan and fry the onion, garlic, and the whole spices (cardamom, star anise, cinnamon, and cloves) for 10 minutes on medium heat, stirring all the time. Add the diced zucchini and cook for 10 minutes on medium heat.

Add the drained rice and mix well, still on medium heat, for 5–7 minutes to dry it.

De-glaze the rice with 2 cups (500 ml) of boiling water. Add the turmeric and diced tomato. Season with salt, stir well, and cover with a lid. Simmer for 15 minutes. Remove the pan from the stovetop and leave to rest for 10 minutes with the lid on, allowing the spices to infuse.

Dry-roast the flaked almonds in a frying pan.

Garnish the rice with the toasted almonds and serve.

For info

Pulao is closely
related to pilaf rice.

Lemon rice
Nimbu pulao

Wash the rice thoroughly and leave it to soak for 15–20 minutes.

Toast the mustard seeds in the oil for 5–7 minutes on medium heat. Add the turmeric and lemon juice, then reduce the liquid by half for 3 minutes on medium heat.

Add the drained rice, salt, and scant 2 cups (450 ml) of water. Cover and cook for 15 minutes on medium heat.

Turn off the heat and leave the rice for 10 minutes with the lid on.

Gently stir the rice and serve immediately.

Preparation: 5 minutes
Resting time:
20 + 10 minutes
Cooking time: 20 minutes

1½ cups (300 g) Basmati rice
1 tsp mustard seeds
½ tsp turmeric powder
juice of 1 lemon
1 tbsp vegetable oil
½ tsp salt

Ingredients to serve 4

Preparation: 10 minutes
Resting time: 10 minutes
Cooking time: 35 minutes

Ingredients to serve 4

1¼ cups (250 g) Basmati rice
1 tsp cumin seeds
9 oz (250 g) fresh young
  spinach
½ tsp turmeric
flaked almonds
vegetable oil
salt

Spinach rice
Palak pulao

Cook the rice in a pan with generous 1½ cups (375 ml) of water and ½ teaspoon of salt. Cover and cook on medium heat for about 18 minutes, following the recipe on page 19.

Turn off the heat. Leave the rice covered in the pan for a further 10 minutes, and fluff it up with a fork.

Fry the cumin seeds in a large frying pan containing 2 tablespoons of vegetable oil for 3 minutes on medium heat.

Add the spinach, turmeric, and ⅓ teaspoon of salt, and wilt the spinach for 3 minutes on high heat.

Add the fluffed-up rice, stir in the almonds, and gently mix the rice through the spinach.

Tip
"Wilting" the spinach simply means cooking it.

Dhal

Yellow lentil curry

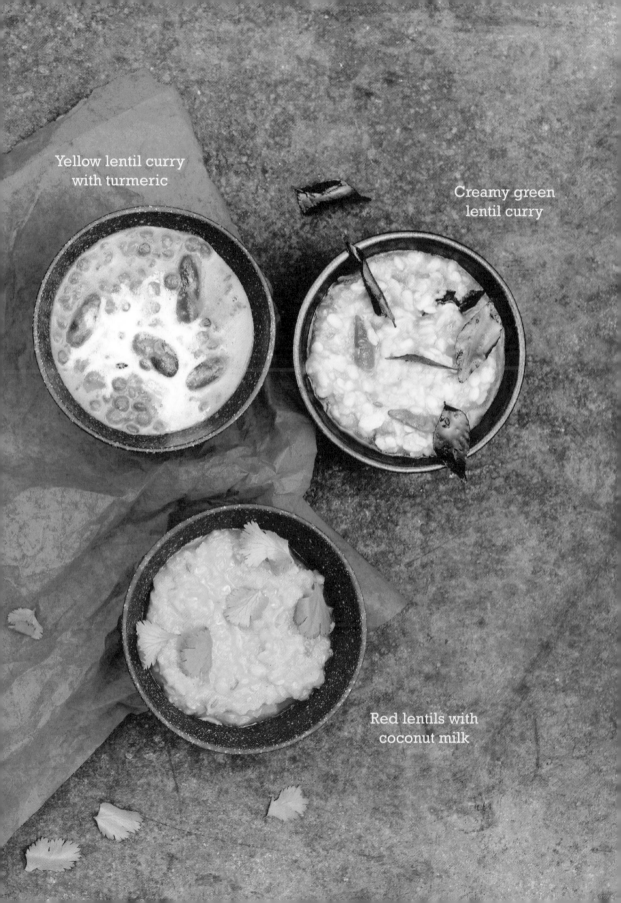

Yellow lentil curry
with turmeric

Creamy green
lentil curry

Red lentils with
coconut milk

Creamy green lentil curry Dahl makhani

Ingredients to serve 4

Preparation: 15 minutes
Cooking time: 50 minutes

¾ cup (150 g) green lentils
1 bay leaf
2 cardamom pods
2 cloves
1 cinnamon stick
1 tsp garlic and ginger paste (see recipe on p. 26)
1 small green chili, de-seeded
1 tbsp ground cumin
1 pinch turmeric
generous ¾ cup (200 ml) tomato paste
½ cup (100 g) cooked kidney beans
7 tbsp (100 ml) half-and-half cream
1 tbsp dried fenugreek leaves (optional)
2–3 sprigs fresh cilantro
2 tbsp vegetable oil
salt

Cook the green lentils in a casserole with 2 cups (500 ml) of water and the bay leaf. It should take 20 minutes on medium heat.

Make the sauce. In a sauté pan, fry the cardamom, cloves, and cinnamon stick in the oil for 10 minutes on medium heat.

Add the garlic and ginger paste, chopped green chili, cumin powder, scant ½ teaspoon of salt, and the turmeric. When the mixture is dry, add the tomato paste, cover with a lid, and cook for 10 minutes.

Add the lentils, cooked kidney beans, cream, and fenugreek. Cover and simmer for a further 10 minutes.

Serve sprinkled with chopped cilantro.

Yellow lentil curry Dahl fry

Preparation: 10 minutes
Resting time: 1–2 hours
Cooking time: 25 minutes

generous 1⅓ cups (200 g) moong dahl (small yellow lentils)
½ tsp turmeric
1 tbsp cumin seeds
3–4 curry leaves
1 onion
1 tomato
1 tsp garlic and ginger paste (see recipe on p. 26)
1 dried red chili (optional)
1 tsp ground coriander
1 pinch red chili powder
1 tbsp vegetable oil or ghee
salt

Soak the lentils in a large pan of cold water for 1–2 hours.

Bring to the boil in 3 times their volume of water (unsalted), add the turmeric, and cook for 10 minutes.

Meanwhile, fry the cumin seeds and curry leaves in the vegetable oil or ghee for 5 minutes on medium heat, until they start to brown. Add the onion and chopped tomato, garlic and ginger paste, whole dried red chili, ground coriander, scant ½ teaspoon of salt, and the chili powder. Cover and cook for 10 minutes.

Add the drained lentils to this mixture.

Moong dahl (yellow lentils) are used for this simple everyday recipe.

Yellow lentil curry with turmeric Tarka dahl

Preparation: 10 minutes
Resting time: 1 hour
Cooking time: 25 minutes

generous 1 cup (150 g) chana dahl (large yellow
    lentils)
½ tsp turmeric
2 tomatoes
1 tbsp cumin seeds
1 pinch asafetida
1 bay leaf
2 small dried chilis
2 garlic cloves
juice of 1 lime
2 tbsp vegetable oil or ghee
salt

Rinse the lentils and soak for 1 hour in cold water. Bring to the boil in 3 times their volume of water, together with the turmeric and chopped tomatoes, and cook for 15 minutes.

Meanwhile, heat the oil or ghee in a pan and sauté the cumin seeds, asafetida, bay leaf, whole dried chilis, and chopped garlic for 10 minutes on high heat until they start to brown.

Add the fried spices to the lentils. Mix well, season with salt, and serve drizzled with lime juice.

"Tarka" indicates that the spices are fried separately and then added to the dish at the end.

Red lentils with coconut milk Coconut masala dahl

Preparation: 25 minutes
Cooking time: 30 minutes

generous 1⅓ cups (200 g) red lentils
2 onions
3 garlic cloves
1 tbsp ground cumin
1 tsp garlic and ginger paste (see recipe on p. 26)
2 tbsp concentrated tomato paste
1 tbsp ground coriander
1 pinch chili powder
1 cup (250 ml) coconut milk
all-purpose flour
2–3 sprigs fresh cilantro
2 tbsp vegetable oil
salt

Rinse the lentils and transfer them to a pan of cold, unsalted water. Bring to the boil and cook for 15 minutes, or until cooked through.

Put the oil into a sauté pan, and fry 1 chopped onion with the cumin for 10 minutes on medium heat.

Add the garlic and ginger paste, tomato paste, ground coriander, chili powder, and 4 tablespoons of water. Mix this curry paste well, and simmer gently for 5–10 minutes.

Add the coconut milk and season with salt. Simmer for 5 minutes, then add the drained lentils. Sprinkle with fried onions (see tip below) and freshly chopped cilantro.

To make your own fried onions, finely slice an onion, dust with flour, and fry in hot (but not smoking) oil.

Vegetarian dishes

There are approximately 480 million vegetarians in India, nearly 40 percent of the total population of 1.2 billion, so there is a plentiful supply of vegetarian recipes! I have included some classics in this book, but as you can imagine, the list could be very much longer.

Mashed eggplant curry
Baingan bartha

Cut the eggplants in half lengthways. Make incisions in the cut side of the eggplant halves, without breaking the skin. Sprinkle with garam masala, and drizzle some oil over the flesh.

Cover the eggplants with aluminum foil to stop them turning black. Bake them in the oven at 355 °F (180 °C) for 25 minutes.

Meanwhile, sauté the 2 crushed garlic cloves in vegetable oil for 5 minutes on high heat.

Add the chopped tomato and salt, and fry for 5 minutes on medium heat. Set to one side.

When the eggplants are cooked, leave them to cool. Scoop out the flesh with a tablespoon and chop it coarsely.

Combine the eggplant flesh, tomato and garlic mixture, yogurt, and a generous handful of freshly chopped cilantro.

Serve with naan bread (see recipe on p. 40).

(see recipe on p. 40)

Preparation: 15 minutes
Cooking time: 25 minutes

2 shiny eggplants
2 tbsp garam masala
2 garlic cloves
1 very ripe tomato
2 tbsp set or creamy yogurt
4–5 sprigs fresh cilantro
vegetable oil
salt

Ingredients to serve 4

Preparation: 15 minutes
Cooking time: 40 minutes

Ingredients to serve 4

¾ lb (350 g) potatoes
¾ lb (350 g) cauliflower
1 tsp black mustard seeds
2 garlic cloves
¾ in (2 cm) piece ginger
  root
1 onion
½ tsp turmeric
1 tsp ground coriander
⅔ cup (100 g) peas (fresh
  or frozen)
4–5 sprigs fresh cilantro
vegetable oil
salt

Potato, cauliflower, and pea curry

Aloo ghobi mattar

Peel the potatoes and dice them into small cubes (approximately ½ in / 1½ cm). Separate the cauliflower into florets of similar size to the potatoes.

Bring a large pan of cold, unsalted water to the boil, and cook the potatoes and cauliflower for about 10 minutes. Set them to one side.

In a sauté pan, fry the mustard seeds in 1 tablespoon of hot oil for 5 minutes on medium heat.

Add the garlic, ginger, and chopped onion. Cook on low heat for 10 minutes, stirring all the time. Add the remaining spices (turmeric and ground coriander), mixing well, and add 7 tablespoons (100 ml) of water. Reduce completely. This should take 7–10 minutes.

Add the cooked potato and cauliflower along with 1¼ cups (300 ml) of water. Cover, and simmer for 20 minutes.

Add the peas and continue to cook for a further 5 minutes on low heat. Sprinkle with freshly chopped cilantro and serve the curry with Basmati rice or chapatis.

As the raw peas are added at the end of the cooking time, they retain their beautiful green color and crunch.

118

Preparation: 15 minutes
Cooking time: 45 minutes

Ingredients to serve 4

7 oz (200 g) paneer (see
  recipe on p. 29)
1 brown onion
2 garlic cloves
1 small piece ginger root
1 small green chili or
  1 pinch hot chili powder
  (optional)
spices: 2 tsp garam masala,
  ½ tsp turmeric,
  1 tsp ground cumin,
  1 tsp ground coriander
generous ¾ cup (200 ml)
  passata
1¼ lb (600 g) fresh spinach
generous ¾ cup (200 ml)
  half-and-half cream
vegetable oil
salt and pepper

Spinach with paneer
Palak paneer

Brown the paneer cubes on all sides in a pan with some oil.

Brown the chopped onions in some vegetable oil for 10 minutes on medium heat. Add the crushed garlic, grated ginger, chopped and de-seeded chili, all the spices, and 7 tablespoons (100 ml) of water. Cook for 10 minutes on medium heat, stirring well.

When the liquid has reduced, add the passata. Simmer gently, uncovered, for about 15 minutes.

Add the raw spinach, coarsely chopped, to this mixture. Simmer for a further 10 minutes, then pour in the cream.

Add the paneer to the curry and serve immediately.

Ingredients to serve 4

7 oz (200 g) paneer
  (see recipe on p. 29)
9 oz (250 g) potatoes
3½ oz (100 g) carrots
3½ oz (100 g) peas
2 tbsp (20 g) all-purpose flour
vegetable oil

For the sauce
1 onion
2 garlic cloves
¾ in (2 cm) piece ginger root
1 tbsp concentrated tomato
  paste
1 tbsp ground coriander
1 tbsp ground cumin
generous 1 lb (500 g) very
  ripe tomatoes (or 1⅔ cups /
  400 ml chopped tomatoes)
3 tbsp (30 g) unsalted
  cashew nuts
7 tbsp (100 ml) half-and-half
  cream
2 tbsp (10 g) butter
4–5 sprigs fresh cilantro
vegetable oil
salt

Vegetable balls with paneer and creamy sauce
Malai kofta korma

Make the vegetable balls: grate the paneer, reserving 1 tablespoon.

Cook the vegetables in salted water, and drain carefully. Mash them coarsely. Combine this mixture with the paneer and flour, and shape it into little balls the size of a walnut. Brown the vegetable balls in 4 tablespoons of very hot (but not smoking) oil for 5 minutes on each side, on medium heat. Set to one side.

Now make the creamy sauce. In a sauté pan, heat 1 tablespoon of oil and sweat the chopped onion, together with the puréed garlic and ginger. Cook for 10 minutes on medium heat, stirring all the time.

Add the tomato paste, coriander, cumin, and 7 tablespoons (100 ml) of water, and reduce the liquid on medium heat for 10 minutes.

Whizz the tomatoes and cashew nuts in a food mixer, then add the creamy sauce. Simmer gently for 10 minutes. Stir in the cream and butter, and simmer gently for a further 10 minutes. Add the vegetable balls to the sauce, then the freshly chopped cilantro and the reserved spoonful of grated paneer.

Serve with Basmati rice.

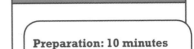

Fried okra
Bhindi masala

Cut off the okra stem ends and slice them lengthways.

Chop the onion, tomato, chili, and bell pepper into equal-size pieces, approximately ⅓ in (1 cm).

Heat 2 tablespoons of oil in a frying pan until very hot (but not smoking). Sauté the okra, onions, pepper, and chili for 10 minutes, stirring all the time.

Add the lime juice, tomato, spices, and salt, and continue to cook for 10 minutes, still stirring.

Remove the pan from the stovetop, sprinkle on the fresh cilantro, and serve immediately.

Okra are also known as gumbo or lady's fingers.

Tip
The lime juice prevents the okra from becoming sticky when cooked.

Preparation: 10 minutes
Cooking time: 20 minutes

generous 1 lb (500 g) okra (gumbo)
1 red onion
1 small firm tomato
½ green chili, de-seeded
1 small red bell pepper
juice of ½ lime
1 tsp ground coriander
1 pinch turmeric
some fresh cilantro
vegetable oil
salt

Ingredients to serve 4

Ingredients to serve 4

1¼ lb (600 g) firm paneer
(see recipe on p. 29)
½ tsp turmeric + 1 extra
pinch
1 onion
2 garlic cloves
¾ in (2 cm) piece fresh
ginger root
1 tbsp concentrated tomato
paste, ground coriander
1 lb (500 g) very ripe
tomatoes (or 1⅔ cups /
400 ml chopped tomatoes)
3 tbsp (30 g) blanched
almonds
7 tbsp (100 ml) half-and-half
cream
2 tbsp (10 g) butter
some fresh cilantro
vegetable oil; salt

Paneer korma

Cut the paneer into even chunks. Brown them in
4 tablespoons of very hot (but not smoking) oil with a
pinch of turmeric for 2 minutes on each side. Drain on
paper towels.

Make the creamy sauce. Sweat the finely chopped onions
and puréed garlic and ginger in 1 tablespoon of oil. Cook
for 10 minutes, stirring all the time.

Stir in the tomato paste, coriander, ½ teaspoon of
turmeric, 7 tablespoons (100 ml) of water, and some salt,
and reduce the liquid.

Whizz the tomatoes and almonds in a food mixer. Add
the spicy tomato sauce. Simmer gently for 10 minutes,
and stir in the cream and butter. Simmer for a further
10 minutes.

Add the paneer chunks to the sauce, and serve with
cilantro leaves and fragrant Basmati rice.

Desserts and drinks

In Indian cuisine desserts are like candy—eaten outside mealtimes, on the go, or in the home when entertaining friends. Also regarded as a symbol of affluence, these sweet dishes are displayed in large heaps and in many forms at parties and weddings.

Fritters with syrup
Gulab jamun

Preparation: 25 minutes
Resting time: 15 minutes
+ 6 hours minimum,
ideally overnight
Cooking time: 10 minutes

Ingredients to serve 4

2 tbsp (20 g) all-purpose flour
¼ tsp yeast
5 tbsp (70 g) butter
1 cup (150 g) milk powder
2 tbsp (25 g) fine durum wheat semolina (soaked in a small amount of hot water)
¼ cup (60 ml) low-fat milk
vegetable shortening

For the syrup
1 tsp lemon juice
7 tbsp (100 ml) water
7 tbsp (100 g) sugar

Combine the flour and yeast in a bowl. Set to one side.

Melt the butter and pour it into a bowl. Add the milk powder, low-fat milk, and flour mix.

Mix in the soaked semolina to make a dough. Leave to rest for 15 minutes.

Meanwhile make the syrup. Heat all the syrup ingredients gently, until a pale golden brown color.

Shape the dough into walnut-size balls. In a pan, fry the little balls in ¾ in (2 cm) hot (but not smoking) vegetable shortening for 10 minutes on medium heat until nice and golden.

Lift them out of the pan with a skimmer, and drain briefly on a plate lined with paper towels. Dip them in the syrup while still warm but not piping hot. Leave them to soak up the syrup for at least 6 hours, ideally overnight.

Serve sprinkled with chopped pistachios.

Make sure you get the temperature of the oil just right. If it is too hot, your gulabs with be burnt on the outside and raw inside. If the oil is not hot enough, they will disintegrate.

Plain lassi

Lassi is the classic refreshing drink to soothe the palate when eating spicy food. It can be made without milk, which makes it easier to digest.

Preparation: 5 minutes

4 small pots whole milk natural yogurt
⅔ cup (150 ml) milk
¼ tsp sugar
1 pinch salt
freshly ground pepper

Whizz all the ingredients in a food mixer and refrigerate for at least 1 hour before serving.

Mango lassi

Preparation: 5 minutes

3 small pots whole milk natural yogurt
7 tbsp (100 ml) milk
generous 2 cups (400 ml) mango pulp
¼ tsp cardamom seeds
1 pinch salt

Whizz all the ingredients in a food mixer and refrigerate for at least 1 hour before serving.

Toffee lassi

Preparation: 5 minutes

4 small pots whole milk natural yogurt
7 tbsp (100 ml) milk
4 tbsp sweetened condensed milk
1 vanilla pod
1 pinch salt

Whisk 1 pot of yogurt with the scraped-
out vanilla seeds and condensed milk,
then whisk in the salt, milk,
and the other 3 yogurts.
Refrigerate for at
least 1 hour before
serving.

Rose lassi

Preparation: 5 minutes

4 small pots whole milk natural yogurt
⅔ cup (150 ml) milk
¼ tsp ginger paste
4 tbsp rose syrup
1 pinch salt

Whizz all the ingredients in a food
mixer and refrigerate for at least 1 hour
before serving.

Ingredients to serve 4

- 1¾ cups (450 g) whipping cream
- 7 tbsp (100 ml) milk
- 4½ tbsp (60 g) sugar
- 1 Madagascar vanilla pod
- 2 jasmine teabags
- 2 sheets gelatin

Panna cotta with jasmine tea

Put the cream, milk, sugar, and vanilla pod with seeds into a pan. Bring to the boil and cook for 1 minute.

Meanwhile infuse the 2 jasmine teabags in 1 cup of very hot water, and discard the water.

Remove the pan from the stovetop, and dip the teabags into the creamy mixture. Cover the pan and leave to infuse for 5–7minutes.

Soak the gelatin leaves in some cold water for 1 minute, then drain. Stir the gelatin leaves through the cream. Remove the vanilla pod and pour the mixture into glasses straight away.

Refrigerate for at least 2 hours.

For info
Make this dessert with your favorite tea.

Almond bonbons
Badam barfi

Whizz the ground almonds in a food mixer with a generous ¾ cup (200 ml) milk to make a smooth cream.

Melt the butter with the cardamom seeds in a frying pan. Add the almond cream and sugar, and heat gently until the sugar dissolves.

Add the rest of the milk gradually, topping up as it reduces.

Thicken the mixture on low heat for about 20 minutes. Gradually it will begin to come away from the sides of the pan. When the mixture has dried up, transfer the almond paste to a square dish and smooth over the top.

Refrigerate and cut into whatever shapes you like.

Sprinkle with shredded coconut.

Preparation: 10 minutes
Cooking time: 20 minutes

2¼ cups (200 g) ground almonds
1 quart (1 liter) whole milk
½ tsp cardamom, seeds or ground
⅔ cup (150 g) sugar
2 tbsp shredded coconut
2 tbsp (10 g) butter or ghee (see recipe on p. 31)

Ingredients to make 6

For info

Barfi, these little almond bonbons, are a type of confectionery called mithaï (Indian sweetmeats) which are usually served with a hot drink or as a snack, rather than as a dessert.

Preparation: 10 minutes
Cooking time: 1 hour
Freezing time: 4 hours
minimum

Ingredients to make 6 kulfis

1 quart (1 liter) whole milk
½ tsp ground cardamom
  seeds
⅔ cup (75 g) confectioner's
  sugar
1⅔ cups (250 ml) heavy
  cream
¼ cup (20 g) ground almonds
4 tbsp rose-flavored syrup
3 tbsp (20 g) chopped,
  peeled pistachios

Rose kulfi
Pista gulabi kulfi

Bring the milk and cardamom to the boil in a pan, stirring frequently.

Turn down the heat; add the sugar, cream, and almonds. Reduce by half, stirring frequently (this takes about 1 hour).

Allow the milk to cool down, and add the rose syrup and half of the chopped pistachios. Mix well, let it cool down, and pour it into the shape of ice-cream mold that you prefer.

Put them in the freezer for at least 4 hours. Serve with chopped pistachios.

It makes it easier to remove the ice cream from the mold if you run it under warm water.
This ice cream is easy to make without an ice-cream maker. Using metal molds helps to conduct the cold.

Banana halva

Ingredients to serve 4

Preparation: 10 minutes
Cooking time: 20 minutes

3½ tbsp (50 g) butter or ghee
1 tsp ground cinnamon
6 tbsp (50 g) raisins
3¼ lb (1½ kg) bananas
3½ tbsp (50 g) sugar
10 tbsp (150 ml) sweetened
    condensed milk

Heat the butter in a pan until it froths. Add the cinnamon and raisins, and simmer gently for 5 minutes.

When the raisins have swollen, add the finely chopped bananas and the sugar. Cook for 10 minutes, lightly mashing the bananas.

Add the condensed milk and simmer gently until the mixture thickens.

Serve warm with some chai, or tea with milk.

MY FAVORITE RESTAURANTS

Nalas Aappakadai Paris
54, rue Louis-Blanc
75010 Paris
Tél. : 01 42 05 50 50

Jaipur Café
17, rue des Messageries
75010 Paris
Tél. : 01 48 01 06 00

Dishoom
12 Upper St. Martin's Lane
London, United Kingdom
www.dishroom.com

Masala Zone
48 Floral Street
London, United Kingdom
www.masalazone.com

INDIAN FOOD ON THE WEB

www.indianfoodsco.com
www.internationalfoodship.com
www.ishopindian.com
www.thespicehouse.com
www.shop.khanapakana.com
www.spicesofindia.co.uk
www.spicemart.co.uk
www.theasiancookshop.co.uk

MY BLOG

www.bollywoodkitchen.com

Huge thanks to my friends and family for their unfailing support since I embarked on my Bollywood Kitchen adventure.
A big thank-you to my editor, Aurélie, for always being available and believing in me, as well as to Sophie and Patrice, whose combined expertise helped to make this dream come true.
I am also grateful to Birgit and Dorian for their sound advice. Warmest thanks to my parents and extended family.
Finally, I cannot thank Julien enough, my strength and support always.
For Jahan and Amina.

© Mango, Paris – 2015
Original Title: *Inde : Toutes les bases de la
cuisine indienne*
ISBN 978-23-17010-04-0

Editorial director: Anne la Fay
Editor: Aurélie Cazenave
Creative directors: Laurent Quellet and Julie Mathieu
Layout: Elfried Werner
Proofreading: Delphine Billaut

© for this English edition: h.f.ullmann publishing GmbH

Translation from French: Ann Drummond, in association
with First Edition Translations Ltd, Cambridge, UK
Overall responsibility for production:
h.f.ullmann publishing GmbH, Potsdam, Germany

Printed in India, 2016

ISBN 978-3-8480-0994-7

10 9 8 7 6 5 4 3 2 1
X IX VIII VII VI IV III II I

www.ullmannmedien.com
info@ullmannmedien.com
facebook.com/hfullmann
twitter.com/hfullmann_int